THE
RECEPTION

BLACK, WHITE, AND GREY

Allyse Bégin

iUNIVERSE, INC.
BLOOMINGTON

The Reception
Black, White, and Grey

iUniverse books may be ordered through booksellers or by contacting:

iUniverse
1663 Liberty Drive
Bloomington, IN 47403
www.iuniverse.com
1-800-Authors (1-800-288-4677)

Because of the dynamic nature of the Internet, any web addresses or links contained in
this book may have changed since publication and may no longer be valid. The views
expressed in this work are solely those of the author and do not necessarily reflect the
views of the publisher, and the publisher hereby disclaims any responsibility for them.

Any people depicted in stock imagery provided by Thinkstock are models,
and such images are being used for illustrative purposes only.

Certain stock imagery © Thinkstock.

ISBN: 978-1-4759-2964-5 (sc)
ISBN: 978-1-4759-2965-2 (e)

Printed in the United States of America

iUniverse rev. date: 6/29/2012

CONTENTS

BLACK AND LIGHT

(INTRO POEM)

You see the world in black and white;

All grey is just perfume.

Your other side of dark is bright,

A consummated tune.

FOREWORD

When it comes to poetry, I have one main influence: my sister. I have had the privilege of writing a couple of experimental poems with her over the last few years, and I thought it would be appropriate to feature them in this collection. Her interest in poetry began at what I would consider an early age.

My sister's work had a certain style that eventually inspired me to begin writing myself. What I can remember of her poetry was mostly written in free verse. At the time she began sharing her work with me, I had not yet realized how personal and emotional the process of writing could be. Suddenly there was a whole new means of expression available to me—saying something without actually saying it. I could finally direct my emotions to create something of substance, and then have the chance to look at it, contain it, control it, and edit it.

Today I consider writing poetry a form of art therapy for times of distress and simply a creative outlet at other times. My poems usually represent my immediate mood at a given time; therefore, the subject matter usually isn't based on my own experiences—it just sets the right mood.

I think I can truly appreciate poetry now that I have lived a little and have learned that expressing myself eases tension, builds creativity, and opens doors to relating to others in uncomplicated ways. I definitely recommend reading and/or writing poetry to anyone with an open mind. There is no limiting, standard form of poem to restrict the flow of creativity. This is important to me as an artist.

All I can really hope for my poetry is that it will entertain a wide audience and inspire others to indulge in writing.

My famous influences include William Shakespeare, Emily Dickinson, and E.E. Cummings, as well as lyricists/songwriters like Leonard Cohen, Billy Corgan, and Paul McCartney, whose work I can *also* thank my sister for introducing into my readings.

Dedicated to Susan Ann Bégin, my guardian angel;
may I, one day, hold your hand in return.

ID

(INSTINCT)

A BANG-BANG,
THAT'S MY MAN

A big bad bang
Shot at close range
A bloody mess
An awful shame

A big bad bang
Another round
A bloody blow
I'm on the ground

A big bad bang
His stranger ways
A bloody shot
The third today

A big bad bang
Like sound-surround
A bloody sin
This gun he found

A big bad bang
He will not change
A bloody grin
Through massive rage

A big bad BANG
My stranger days
A bloody end
Through red hot haze

A RELENTLESS
EFFORT FOR NONE

Michelle is blessed and quite profound,
She's witnessed stress and found it sound,
She's loved at best on solid ground,
Yet still she's rather wound.

Her mind is quick, but still a guest,
Wraps scissors in her hands to jest;
She'd rather run them through her chest,
Yet slowly comes around.

BECAUSE I LEFT ...

And in the middle of my reflection
I cast a stone.
I cast what was not mine
So it held onto my palm.

Against the shoreline and the vast separation
That brought me to the conclusion that,
Although her sun may rise,
It fell—
I sat in a hole, whose castle had gone with the tide.

Its memories were good for what they were worth,
But the value of *my* time
Was shaded in the moment of truth.

It's in truth that I find it hard to believe
That my reflection had continued to thrive,
even in my absence.

So when I gaze into my ocean's surface to catch a glimpse
Or to catch wind of a song,
Don't blame me if I feel the weight on my palm,
Because it's not only pain,
It's the reflection that I never knew.

BLUE TEARS ON HORIZON

Sunrise
Some rise
Some fall
Even through it all
Sunset
We met
And now
Some how
I can't react
To stay intact
Lunar
Sooner or
Later still
A bashful will
A bitter rant
An always "can't"
My lonely self
You sought to shelf
I'll shake the dust
Till dawn's new dusk
I'll pain
For you
All stained
In blue

'BOUT A MAN

I was thinking the colour green/
He had two hands,
Stained with ... it upon
Was the moonlit hour)
In palms
Gathering
Water drops fell; they twisted
i think ITS raining –
it is raining
but it looks like mud.
It is mud ...

And then he said with much relief
"I can think of only to batter my eyelashes"
The street lamp flickered as he
Pa(ss)ed : dimming our souls
Thus
thus
the green was sorrow, but the rain washed clean
-repenting'
And with a quick squint
He read about a man.

(Featuring Genesia Bégin)

CEMENT YOUR TEETH

I drew a line that granted time,
And on the other side I'd fly
To reach my shameful concubine;
It gave my innocence a high.

The morning sneezed a wicked blue
That caught your eye then plunged into,
To snatch the bait while falling through;
It wasn't late, just overdue.

My dying friend with painted toes
Left gadgets in my bed to sew,
And on his death I pained to know
They had procured my only foe.

DON'T KILL THE MESSENGER

Dear shady, short reaction—
Be back in 5.

Meanwhile, with a particularly [cautious], [foolish], [naughty] grin,
I let you in.

FOURTEEN

I'm filing my dreams
To number fourteen,
I'm hoping I'll finish tonight.

They're rather obscure,
Completely a blur,
Yet lucid whilst I'm tucked in tight.

HOW CONVENIENT

Savour love, no need to cater;
Riches coast and lack in favour.
Step in line, don't be a hater,
Lick the folly lolly flavour.

True content is pen and paper.
Build your dreams on empty wagers,
Tempting tides, the bridge is safer;
Live to grease your agitator.

Muscles ache to aid thy neighbour,
Young at heart, our great creator;
Cross your eyes to see my failure,
Reach inside and see me later.

I WILL AT LEAST

/This/ as it is
    at least foR mE
        is what I can do give take
for))))you (ponder(ed
So defiant is my Maker is why

I am alone at love
I am not *home* my love
!
Alas you smile
    that smile resists for it exists for /This/

        and This as it was atleastforyou a phenomenon
ofanother kind
The Goings come back They come
      if me you s e e e eeyes
that's all the n.o.w. I need (SHOUT(ED
So high is my Maker is high

I am a pawn in love …
I wrote it in a *song* my love
""for you my love comes chea-P oops I mean free,
.but words are only cheap

I'LL FIND WITHIN

And yet, with Summer come and gone,
Winter casts its desolate shadow too soon;
Who knew Death to be so beautiful
and placid
(shamefully so).
Who knew Death to be so bold
and impartial
(willfully so).
Who knew Death to be so cold
and cunning
(painfully so).
And so, with each a shadow cast,
Winter—I'll find within

Something to end my desolate shadow too.

LIBERATION

I have a spastic shadow =
I'm due for an operation;
It walks on stucco ceilings
This makes for
They think
This makes up for wasted space.
Trailing is a messy filling of contorted drawings—
In hastened pace—this makes up for wasted time.
It's standing under doorways;
{Cracks,ledges}edging ever so closer.
wE turns circle, in circles, and I felt giddy when I went to the nurse
But she pricked me a needle or two and my shadow needn't be
-We turn and finally I can can see-

The Nazareth.
Sound is round, but completely misleading
How not—unfair, hey!
My shadow beat me there.
The doctor with the light
Open
Close
Open ... close

Last circle we go
Spun, Squinting far, I've lost count. .
The purple or were they purple or were they?
Kiss [say] it.
I'm eyes directed in another.

(Featuring Genesia Bégin)

ONE ON THE LEFT
AND ON THE RIGHT

When I began the puncture,
Before I fed the cause,
A thought was left enraptured;
Two thoughts were hidden flaws.

One on the left and on the right.

A fourth of endless, buried chains,
A fifth was thought to've rot;
One was for the pleasure—blurred,
Which now I've too forgot.

All rights possessed too keen of sight.

The seventh blindly lost the eighth,
Whose shadow fits my own,
I knew the numb defeat would pass
With nine compiled bones.

When left to bare, they sought to flight.

I thought of you, (my puncture wound)
My tenth and lasting role,
The nerve to twitch the final stretch;
Effect will bind the hole.

The mocking song that killed the night.

RAIN MAN

The Rain Man landed
In the dawn of what was mine.
I fell ill, and so
He came to swallow my breath.
That breath was mine,
But now I'm equally kind.

"After you" he said,
As he tipped his hat and lowered his heart.
A moment passed and with it, my apprehension.
I was sure to fancy a walk with a man who stood in the balance
Of two unlikely masses, if only for a short while.

I wouldn't apologize for my appearance,
And I told him this,
And I told him because I was chilled and restless,
Which made him laugh and hold my hand
Because I didn't know the way—
Then again, he would never mention the end.

I would like to look into his eyes.
When he's a Rain Man
He's smiling
With his eyes pulled shut.
He said, "I'll open my eyes if you open yours first."
I put his hand in mine once more, but he kept on smiling.

The Rain Man sounded
On the street where I remain enclosed within my dawn.
I remain on that street because I'm dreaming of our walk.

I'm sure he'll wait for me, but just in case, I brought an
    umbrella.
I've another hour before I have to catch the train,
And I'd like it if I was well enough to say goodbye.

SURFACE MOURN

Holding still—
Two tattered bones
Incongruent-
ly Adorned
In zippers
Laden; patch the skin—
Whose livelihood
Proves paper thin
(This gives way to
Few bitter minds,
Whose blacker hearts
Impress me blind).

THE NOTHINGNESS
I'VE COME TO SHARE

(My Dream)

In all my dreams
Of coffin breeze
Borne mangled trees
Who caught disease.

But never more
Of thoughts were born,
Until the sore
Of you, I bore.

Your entrance swift,
As was your slip,
But so to shift,
You took a lift.

You dangled there,
Your whimsy hair
All fire flare,
In worn despair.

The churning pain
Through torrent rain;
The seething bane,
The strain remains.

I held your hand
Beneath the sand,
And reaching, ran,
My struggle planned.

With hands I fed,
I've gone unsaid;
With courage bred,
I left you dead.

Now fallen down,
Your limbs around;
The tattered ground
Will hold you sound.

The haunting bliss,
Your floating mist;
I gave you this,
The nothingness.

THE TIN MAN

The Tin Man's empty pail
His elements fail
Forever just a stove top
Sounds like a road block

The Tin Man's gaping hole
See how far it goes
Drop a quarter down his well
Sounds like a cow bell

The Tin Man's missing beat
No one left him on repeat
He's fast asleep, no "tick-tock"
Sounds like a "stop ...watch"

The Tin Man's barren drum
No echo "tum tum"
His hollow heaves a huge sigh
Sounds like a war cry

WEIRD ENDINGS

Another one down
What a shame
Touched by the hand of originality
"There *ain't no* UP-SIDE of DOWN"
Yes, that's exactly where they stay
Another one found
Observed, befriended
And there, as clear as ever
The end appeared
So unforgiving
So unfortunate
So now I've gained no trust and lost nothing in return
Perhaps more than I'm willing to part with
But nothing I'm willing to accept
Another one down
Then reappears for a second round
Oh how I love a good secret
If only you had given me a chance to consider
A reaction
A response
Preparation is my better side
My better side I'll have you know
Gives yours a second go
Relentless I suppose
Till one day I'll just let it be
And let it go
And after all of that
You learn it's just the beginning.

WHENCE IN THE LIGHT OF WINCED

Test the holiness of my T-shirt,
The only holiness about me
And it is about (surrounds) me.
As it peels, it is off;
The static cling.

You ARE
The wholeness you bring.
The harness;
The bare back exposed
In the light of (it dawned)
A hole, and the whole time I pondered—
"what eyes look upon Or
What eyes move across"
"But the last line should be 'the static cling'"

The static cling
(was not meant to be).

(Featuring Genesia Bégin)

EGO

(LOGIC)

ABANDONED

Curious rays revealing a chance,
Filling the sky, and through the trees, dance.
Thickly, with twigs and leaves, it is covered,
To dawn's early creatures who've yet to discover.

Speckled and dull, and painted with earth:
Some layers of shell disguising a birth.
Awaiting a moment that's soon to unfold;
A breath of fresh air, a world to behold.

CHILD

I asked her, in her tiny bed
While covering her toes,
If any lasting words, unsaid,
Would carry out in oath.

Her wrinkled nose in painful pose,
She turned to face my own.
A dainty little folded note,
She placed into my hold.

But as her breath kept dry, she died,
No subtlety shone through;
Nothing left to recollect,
No substance but the truth.

Behind me not a word was drawn
But in this lasting reach.
With hesitation come and gone
I so began to read:

"Dry your eyes and with your fingers
Wrap my body, soft and limber,
Or Release my ashes before the winter
(Scatter them in clay)."

I asked her, from her tiny lips,
The need to be alone,
If any lasting words, unsaid,
Would carry out in oath.

Her gentle eyes, in pity, smiled;
She turned and gestured *no*.
And followed still, with all her will
She forced at me a note.

But when no words gave birth, she died;
No sunny days shone through.
Nothing left but to repent,
No substance like the truth.

Behind me, with the curtains drawn,
I felt the teardrops bleed.
With hesitation come and gone
I so began to read:

"When Spring comes thaw, come with your two hands,
Plant lilies, daisies, roses and
Placed in the earth they'll form to stand,
To feed me sun and rain."

COVES OF BATTERED ROCK

With eyes, should perish
Empty thoughts upon the shore,
Fore death doth blindfold.

COVER-SHOCK

Cover-shock a decent few
Whose tidings grew;
Chose more,
Wasting less and standing sore.

Tolerance at full exhaust
Whose gracious thought
Taught less
Essential happiness.

EVERYONE IS TEMPORARY

Everyone is temporary.

In a truthful sense,
That's cheap; that's cheating.

In a more decorated sense,
It's thrilling and more than that,
It's inviting.

In a practical understanding,
The more temporary the experience,
The more experience
There is to be had.

Temporary is,
Quite literally speaking,
The obvious conclusion
(Though left to speculation);
Cradle to coffin.

In a slightly more
Metaphorical sense,
Temporary is based on influence
Whose own influence
Desires/is change;
Change is inevitable.

Revised, it might read:
"Everyone in *my* life is temporary,"
And being as such,

It is of course, relative
To my own understanding.
This then brings me to wonder
How to deal with more permanent bodies/figures.
Well, what could be said,
And has been proven more often than not,
Is that commitment leads to tragedy;
A long-term relationship
With an abuser and their own
Self-inflicting punishment,
In which they seem
So inclined to share ...that's cheap ...that's cheating ... that's why
    everyone is temporary.

GOOD DAY CHECK LIST

Good luck
She gave you strength
—And then some

Big trip
It goes without saying
—Useless

Ugly, bad
Thoughts that stick
—Avoid this

HYPOTHETICALLY
SPEAKING

When I didn't know what it was,
It could have been anything.

Hypothesis:

It would be easy to understand

Observation:

Because it didn't have to be the same thing twice

Conclusion:

Therefore, automatically accepted.

IRON GATE

Pushing through the iron gate
(At North-East corner Queen):
The sun of early Morning,
And on the dew drops, gleam.

ODE TO AUTUMN

Ode to Autumn's cold embrace,
Held against a twisted flame.
Loosely blowing wisps of lace
Impossible to tame.

Your masterpiece, in hastened pace,
Is laden with admired fame;
Disguising true, untainted grace
Of nakedness to shame.

SURREAL

The majesty of time
Lives to nurture all.

TRUTH BE TOLD

A broken soul is a heart's discontent;
A broken heart is a dishonest soul.

UNDISCIPLINED

If I should pocket this emotion,
I must consider the hole.

YESTERDAY-TODAY

Play, lay, say, stay; without delay, be on your way,
For everything grows fainter in the dying light of day.

YOU WAITED IN PATIENCE

Against the dew-drop
Emerald you
Saw the venom
Orchid drew.

Along the bank
They staggered through;
Those sliver fins,
Those silver-blues.

Where once the sun,
Now stood the moon;
The white of light
The night diffused.

The wakenin' owl
Behind you knew,
Yet questions ever—
Always "who?"

Where sky meets earth,
A fogging fume;
Its dulling grey
To calm the loon.

Of yellow buzz;
The bumble tune,
Sits stirring in
The month of June.

The crickets shrill,
And fail to swoon;
Black soulful spies
Fall back too soon.

You listen keen,
The timely queue;
Your breathing held,
So not to move.

It's whisper faint,
"To you adieu"
The forest dies,
And sighs for you.

SUPER-EGO

(MORALITY)

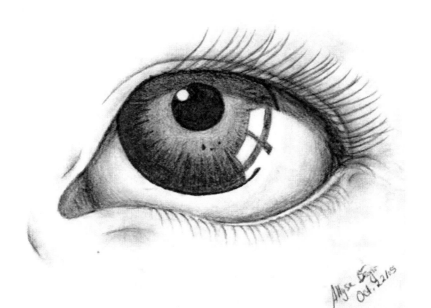

AND SHE WALKS
WITHOUT TALKING

And she walks without talking;
Her lips bent in a curl
As she crosses the street
In her fake vintage fur.

And she models a felt cap:
Pearl-white ribbons and lace.
She sports buttons and seashells,
Each one holding its place.

And she's lost in a daydream
While she sings out of tune;
Her eyes peeled so not to miss
The clown selling balloons.

And she's spotted him standing
In his weather-worn suit,
With his orange faded haircut,
And elongated boots.

And she greets him with smiles,
A short curtsy, a wink,
Then hands him three quarters
For a parrot in pink.

And she watches attentive,
As he folds and he twists,
And then when it's complete
He attaches her wrist.

And she thanks him with pleasure,
So he waves "Come again."
And she walks without talking
As she turns 'round the bend.

BEACH SAND

The little dying stream of light,
So 'trepid in the night.
Rain strumming on my hooded friend,
Who's holding on for life.
We're entering "no trespassing,"
We're climbing off my bike;
It's time to climb that hill again,
Make run, make jump, make flight!

BEAUTY

To all that is beautiful, not always pure;
To beauty divine, and all the obscured;
To rhythmical rhymes, and those who lack tune;
To stunning sea shores, and tumbling dunes;
To those who strike you as pleasantly sweet;
To grace and glamour with delicate feet;
To those who are left with nothing to say;
To pleasantly pink, to presently grey;
To sizes at large, and those who stand tall;
To sizes that count as nothing at all;
You can not imagine the beauty divine,
The imperfectly pure you leave trailing behind.
You can not imagine what truth can unfold
With beauty that's deeper than one can behold.

CRANBERRIES AND BLISSFULNESS

Cranberries and Blissfulness
Pouting baby butter lips
'Round the corner Edward trips
With tattered knees to bare

Bless the button, sew the stitch
Clean your ears behind the itch
Find a chair to reach the switch
An inch or two to spare

EASY LISTENING

I will love as long as I can hate,
I will love as common as I hate,
I will love as passionately as I hate,
I am more determined to hate you than to love you,
I am more jealous to love you than to hate you.

I accept that you will love me,
And you might love me,
But you may hate me,
And you will render me into a state of confusion
When I cannot make a clear distinction of the two.

I hope you know sometimes I do mean it,
And sometimes I will fight it,
And sometimes I'm alone,
And sometimes I'm with sorrow,
And sometimes I'm just ugly.

When I can taste it in the air,
And it is bitter on my tongue,
And I can't bare it through my teeth,
And you stare blankly in my eyes,
I will claim this disdain.

But I hope that you've seen me when I'm laughing,
Because sometimes I'm just joking;
Because sometimes I am real.
And sometimes I am plenty,
And sometimes I am the most beautiful colours,
And sometimes I am—with or without you.

FIRST CAME THE FROST

A heart was stole
With the coming cold;
All through the night she wept.
To bear the guilt
She bends to wilt;
The blue Forget-Me-Not.

Unsightly frail,
And slightly stale;
The Frost came first to say.
Her petals: rust.
The pain adjusts;
The blue will stray to grey.

Her eyes sewn shut,
Her head to tuck
Beneath the thriving shade.
The snow will fall
To hide them all
Beneath a winter's grave.

FLAKES

Frozen figures found fixated;
Focusing forward, feeling flustered.
Fellow followers frequently freeze.
Furiously falling frosted flowers force forth.

Frustrated, failing forecasts fade.
"Fine fiasco!" finds fitting.

GRAVITY

(The Miscarriage)

The life a mother gave, neglecting fear,
Be that of which hath turned 'round and doth stole
The very thing she cherished and held dear;
This gentle soul hath dug a ghastly hole.

The graceful path the helpless angel strode,
Hath shattered into shards of reckless blades.
The tainted light which once so holy glowed;
Young fallen spirit's struggle slowly fades.

Sweet, lonely children's love shall mend thy wing;
Lift up thy naked palms with great despair.
On High, the broken angel's voice will sing.
Through Heaven's door we place her in your care.

The hole shall heal like open wounds through time;
The shattered path forms stairs for you to climb.

GREEN EYES

(INNOCENCE)

Upon the breasts of innocence
An incoherent ignorance;
Green eyed, pale,
So faintly frail,
Sat mustering obedience.

Upon her brow, deliverance,
And shining, shone benevolence;
A sighed relief,
A strong belief
Of simple, quaint equivalence.

Upon her stare of imprudence,
A stranger born in silence;
His hands of warts,
His face contorts,
Embracing life's magnificence.

HARDCOPY

So keep your distance from denial
We'll bury it in sand

Keep your face in all its grace
Not buried in your hands

Do not linger on regret
You're blacking out the truth

Do so love me with forget
To keep you in your youth

Forgive me; forgive yourself
You'll feel it's good to choose

Forgive it just a little
It helps distinguish you

Yesterday I saw you smile
I keep it with me now

So let me know when you're not well
I'll bring it back somehow

HOPE LIE DOWN

Broken morning,
Release the filthy fog
And bathe the flutter-bird in butter-wine.

Broken heaven,
Lay down my hope
And release the morning word in due time.

MIND OF ANOTHER

To indulge myself in the majesty of mind,
At the peak of imagination will I linger;
Through the barrier of reality to find,
Though I try, I can not so much as lay a finger.

MR. HERO

You should never be attracted
To a woman when she's crying
(For attention)
It's loud and depressing and she'll only bring you sorrow
That goes for you too, Mr. Hero

You should join a woman when she's laughing
You should join her when she smiles
Because a woman will cry
No doubt she will cry
Men should cry too, but some women do it for you

NOT TODAY

I took a second breath today,
              and got dressed to find
    I couldn't face the world.
Where I took my travels,
    nothing convinced me more
to close
my eyes and wait
                    for the second sun of tomorrow.

POOR JUDGEMENT
FROM A HYPOCRITE

All of those
And all of that
All who cope
And all who lack

All the ups
And all the downs
All the trips
Are all profound

All of these
And all of this
All the time
Is all I miss

All my friends
Are all the same
`Cause all of them are
All to blame

PREPARED

And here's how much I love you
And here's how much I'll cry
And here's how far I'll be from you
By age of 25

'Cause this is how I'm seething
'Cause this, my life, goes by
'Cause this is how I'm pleasing
But not how hard I try

My wheels inside are turning
My plan has many roads
My passion may be useful
We'll see how far it goes

And that is satisfaction
And that is knowing me
And there's the confirmation
Of my spontaneity

So this is how I'm changing
So this is how I'll grow
So in my heart I love you
Yet this you've always known

Goodbye is not the meaning
Goodbye is for hello
Goodbye to start my journey
But not to be alone

I know it's hard to leave you
I know, you know, it's true
However far my travels
Just know my home's with you

STORY OF A BRIDE

She brushed my hair and kissed my cheek and held me for a while.
I slipped into my wedding gown, she stood back to admire.

He took my side and full of pride, he led me down the aisle.
He shared with me a moment's glance then gave away his child.

I found her there with shaky hands, yet with her doting eyes,
She held her tears and gave a wink and took from me my flowers.

And all at once your eyes met mine, relieved, I heaved a sigh.
Then came our vows, our here-and-nows and "forever we'll abide."

You told me that I made you laugh; I said that you were mine.
I vowed to love but not to lie; you vowed you would provide.

With butterflies, "I do," "I do," and "You may kiss the Bride,"
You took my hand, and then my heart, and with your kiss I smiled.

The crowd closed in, the toasts were made, the guests began to dine.
As music played, we took the floor; your loving arms to guide.

And as we danced you came in close "Melissa, I can't lie,
I would give up *anything*; I will *love you* till I die."

THE CEMETERY WALK

To pass the time,
I passed the streets,
I passed with timid, humble feet.

To hear my heart,
I heard the rain,
I heard it drowning in my pain.

To bear a load,
I bared my past,
I bared my secrets, should they last.

To dream at night,
I dreamt of two,
I dreamt in numbing, knowing you.

To my content,
My own demise,
Myself should sense you stood beside.

To see it now,
I saw it clear,
I saw myself, through you, I fear.

To share the loss,
I shared my soul,
I shared with you a 6-foot hole.

To open hearts,
I opened wounds,
I opened songs with broken tunes.

To want it all,
I wanted this,
I wanted what you wouldn't miss.

To miss, you say?
I missed the queue,
I missed the call, "I'm starting new."

To say hello,
I said goodbye,
I said this 'cause you didn't try.

To leave me now,
You left me cold,
You left my open wounds of old.

To help the pain,
I helped myself,
I helped the mirror off the shelf.

To look inside,
I looked, and smiled,
I looked like such a troubled child.

To will it now,
I would not fall,
Would my reflection chance it all?

To have my own,
I have my truth,
I have my life to think it through.

To goodness lost,
The good shines through,
The good, the bad, and ugly you.

(Now)
To him I love,
He makes me brave,
He heals the things you couldn't save.

(But still)
To you, I thank,
Your life met mine,
The thought of you will pass in time.

To just move on,
I justly say,
I just wanted to finally say

For one last time,
For it must end,
Goodbye again, (a substitute)
A friend.

TUCKED IN TIGHT

Well deep within this bundled sight
That's wrapped so neat, that's tucked in tight,
Are angel wings, and angel toes,
And angel eyes, an angel nose.
Whose hair is golden woven strands,
Who has two grabbing, outstretched hands.
His natural pouting butter lips;
He's breathing as though taking sips.

And deeper still within this boy
Is heart that beats and laughs with joy.
His body moves without a choice
While sleeping, when he hears your voice.
He yearns for your sweet tender care,
The overwhelming love you share.
So when you're whispering *"Goodnight,"*
Remind him that he's tucked in tight.

US TWO

There's only one
Of me (I've checked);
Just me, myself,
And I, and yet—

How nice to think
In matching pairs,
The similar that
common shares.

"I understand"
Means "I relate."
How more than one
Negotiates.

The knowledge of
(And all the while)
"Yes, I'm bluffing
Through my smile."

Two minds at work,
Two hearts unfold,
Two flinging, outstretched
Arms to hold.

One laughing hard,
Two laughing, cry;
Two sets of tears
For happy eyes.

Two of a kind,
Through separate lives.
One step ahead,
Two pasts behind.

I'm here for you
Time and again:
A helping hand,
A loving friend.

I'm here to help
You learn in time,
The pleasure was
(and always) mine.

YOU SAID CHEESE

When given the strange, unusual ways
Of auspicious nights and lyrical days.

One wouldn't deny the stranger of two
Exist among stars and dwell on the moon.

A trick of the light, their gases burn bright,
They radiate wishes and masses of might.

Our ambient, mystical, peek-a-boo tease
That circles the earth and cultivates cheese.

The dippers make home to holes in the sky,
From northern west coasts to southern east-tides.

The moon (or Houdini to credulous eyes):
An ashtray with burn holes that vary in size.

Each astral delight hosts lifelong parades,
Yet by early dawn, their brilliance fades,

And as for our lunar, lone, lingering friend,
Its transition: seamless, both time and again.

CPSIA information can be obtained at www.ICGtesting.com
Printed in the USA
LVOW080343251012

304315LV00001B/8/P

9 781475 929645